PRACTICE READERS
VOLUME 2: UNITS 3 & 4

PEARSON

Glenview, Illinois • Boston, Massachusetts • Chandler, Arizona • Hoboken, New Jersey

ISBN-13: 978-0-328-79573-4
ISBN-10:   0-328-79573-9
6 7 V0B4 18 17 16

Table of Contents

The Table Tennis Tournament

by Gregory Suleman

Suffixes -ian, -ist, -ism

comedian	pessimist	semifinalist(s)
optimism	Russian	stoicism
optimist(s)		

The Junior World Table Tennis Championship was getting under way. This was my third time to compete in the tournament, which brought kids from all over the world to compete. Last year I was a semifinalist in my division, but I lost to a Russian boy named Sergei. It turned out OK, though, because Sergei and I became good friends and still chat a lot on the computer. Sergei made it to the finals, of course, but he lost his round, too, after an exciting match. I could tell he was disappointed, but he took it really well and showed a lot of stoicism. I was really impressed that he could keep his cool when he had come so close to winning the championship.

Sergei was competing in the tournament again this year, and I was looking forward to seeing him. We found each other just a few minutes before the opening ceremony.

"I am wondering, Kyle, if you still have all of your American optimism," Sergei asked, grinning.

"Of course," I said. "How about you?"

"Me, I am always the pessimist," Sergei said, pretending to frown. "That is how I keep from being disappointed."

We laughed, parted ways, and went to our places for the start of the competitions. I chuckled to myself because Sergei pretended to be very serious, but he was a bit of a comedian too. I hoped we would get to see each other more during the competition.

As the tournament went on, both Sergei and I played really well and advanced through each round. At the end of the first day, we were both slated to play in the semifinals, but not against each other. Before we went to our hotel rooms, Sergei found me and wished me luck. The next day was going to be very exciting!

At this tournament, the semifinalists don't play their rounds simultaneously. One pair of opponents plays at a time so that all the spectators can watch the excitement. I watched Sergei play his opponent. It was the best table tennis match I had ever seen. Sergei had some moves I had never even imagined, much less tried! In the end, Sergei was the victor. Then I played my opponent. It was an intense match, but my optimism actually carried me through, and I won my match too. That meant Sergei and I would face each other in the final round. We tried to joke around and chat during the break, but we were tense, and I wondered if our friendship would survive this tournament.

When the round began, we both played really well. It was the best match I'd ever played, but Sergei was a tough opponent, even tougher than the previous year. Sergei scored first and stayed ahead of me the whole match. There in the final round, Sergei beat me for the second time and became the junior world champion. I was awfully disappointed, but I followed Sergei's example and kept my chin up because I didn't want to put a damper on Sergei's exciting moment. Besides, a silver medal was still something to be really proud of, especially since I knew I had played my best game ever.

After the award ceremony, Sergei came to shake my hand again. "Perhaps now we should switch," he said, noticing my returning frown. "I'll be an optimist this year, and you can be the pessimist." I laughed, which made me feel much better.

"No, let's both be optimists for a change," I said. "But you should know that next year it will be my turn to take home the gold."

"Next year," Sergei said, "I will be proud to put that medal around your neck myself."

Yes, I thought happily, our friendship would survive.

Serfs and Peasants in the Middle Ages

by Chris Traylor

**Suffixes *-ian*, *-ist*, *-ism*

feudalism   musicians   realists

guardians

Have you ever daydreamed about being a knight charging around on his horse, perhaps winning a joust as the crowds cheer you on? Some of our ideas about that era are very exciting and romantic. But life in the Middle Ages wasn't exactly comfortable or pleasant all of the time. That was especially true if you weren't lucky enough to be a wealthy landowner.

During the Middle Ages, most people in Europe lived in a feudal system. Under feudalism, a few landowners controlled all the land. They controlled the lives of the people who lived on the land as well. These people—called serfs—weren't slaves exactly. Nevertheless, they couldn't leave to find other work, nor could they buy or sell any property or get married without the permission of the landowner. They were required to work for the landowner for a certain number of days each year. They also had to pay taxes for the right to go on living and working there. They weren't necessarily unhappy with this life. There simply weren't a lot of other choices.

Some peasants were free, but for the most part they too lived on a landowner's property and paid rent. That rent was usually a certain portion of their crops. They had more freedom to choose a career and make their lives better. Some chose to be musicians and performers, blacksmiths, bakers, and so on. Still, they were realists. They knew that living on a landowner's property gave them more protection than they might have had otherwise, so they stayed and paid their taxes just as the serfs did. Those taxes enabled a landowner to employ knights as guardians of his property—and of the people on it.

Going Meatless

by Carolyn Macey

Suffixes *-ian*, *-ist*, *-ism*

vegetarian(s)	dietician	realistic
vegetarianism	moralists	skepticism
physician		

Millions of people around the world practice vegetarianism, or not eating meat. Some do this because of religious beliefs. Others choose it because they love animals. Some moralists say eating animals is wrong. Others are vegetarians because meat is simply not available. Some consider it a luxury item that they choose not to buy. Some make a choice to be vegetarian for health reasons. Whatever reason people have for choosing to live without meat, they have found ways to make nutritious, filling foods.

Vegetarian diets can be very rich in vitamins and protein. The key is variety. The more different kinds of fruits, vegetables, grains, beans, and nuts you can fit in, the more complete the nutrition. Some vegetarians include milk products and eggs in their diet. Other vegetarians choose to live completely without any animal products, including leather and silk fabrics.

If you've never tried vegetarian living, set your skepticism aside and give it a try. Talk to your parents about going meatless for a week. You and your family might talk to a physician or dietician first. He or she can help you make realistic food choices to make sure you get the best nutrition. At the end of the week, dive into a nice steak if that sounds good to you. But who knows? Maybe after a meat-free week, vegetarianism will feel like a good lifestyle choice for you.

Under the Sea

by Renée McLean

Latin Roots *aqua, dict*

aquamarine	aquatic	predict
aquarium	dictated	

When her older sister went away to college, Meiko finally got her wish. She got a bedroom of her own. Her parents gave her permission to paint and decorate it however she wanted, which she had always wanted to do. There were so many possibilities, and no way to predict how it would turn out!

Meiko spent all of her free time browsing Web sites that showed different colors and themes for bedrooms. She wasn't interested in having a frilly, pink, girly room, nor did she want cartoon characters or flowers. She was looking for something that was unique and expressed what was special to her. Nothing on the Web sites really grabbed her attention. She came up blank when she searched at the local library too. She was beginning to wonder if she should just settle for white walls and the same old boring pictures and posters. Then she went on a field trip, and the choice became clear.

Her class went to see the city aquarium. The different exhibits and shows fascinated Meiko. It was hard to know where to look, because everything was so fun to watch. Beautiful fish flitted around in one tank. Playful porpoises showed off in another. A killer whale rose to the surface of one pool and blew water from his blowhole. Seals splashed around in another pool. Her favorite part, she decided, was a glass hallway that actually went through one of the aquarium pools. Standing in that hallway, she was surrounded by the shimmery blue of the water and the flashes of darting fish. She felt like she was under the ocean, with the sun filtering down through the water. She was a little surprised to look up and see a beluga whale staring at her through the glass, as though she was part of an interesting exhibit and he was the visitor. It was a magical moment.

Meiko decided to bring the wonderful feeling from the aquarium back home with her, right into her bedroom! That evening her parents took her to pick out the perfect paint to bring her idea to life. The aquatic theme dictated that the colors should be blues and greens. She found a shade of aquamarine that she absolutely loved.

The next weekend Meiko got to work. She covered all her furniture and other things with a drop cloth, prepared her paint and equipment, and began painting. She was at it for hours and so caught up in the work that she almost forgot about lunch. She started with a coat of the aquamarine, which was pretty but not quite as alive as what she had experienced at the aquarium. She carefully added light streaks of different blues and greens to create depth. The effect was very nice, as it seemed to shimmer and move like the water had at the aquarium. Then she added other underwater details. She stood in the middle of the room and felt the same wonder she had experienced in that underwater hallway. The blue-green walls were teeming with colorful fish, and graceful corals and waving seaweed rose up from the floor. And there in the middle of one wall floated a curious beluga whale.

Meiko cleaned up the equipment, cleared away the drop cloths, and moved her furniture back into place. Then she called her parents in to see the final effect. When they came in, they brought a surprise with them: a new aquarium for her aquatic-themed room.

Long Live Roman Architecture!

by Cathy Thom

> **Latin Roots *aqua*, *dict***
>
> aqueduct(s)   dictated   predictably

The Roman Empire at one time controlled a large part of the known world. Its influence was felt in the British Isles, France, and Germany. Spain and North Africa were under Roman rule. The Middle East and Central Asia were subject to Rome. Roman rulers dictated the laws and customs of these far-flung places. Tough Roman soldiers kept people obedient to the rule of Rome. Rome even tried to make these places *look* Roman. Extensive building projects carried Roman architecture to these "uncultured" outposts. In spite of its great power, the Roman Empire slowly crumbled, and Roman rule predictably came to an end. However, evidence of Roman influence still exists. None is more striking than the beautiful, durable architecture of the Roman aqueducts, bridges, and road systems.

Roman design of waterways was a technological wonder. An amazing system of aqueducts and pipes brought abundant clean water into the city of Rome. One aqueduct actually carried water from springs 90 miles away. The same technology was put to use in the Roman colonies. One breathtaking example can be seen in Nimes, France. With many arches and the typical tiered design, the Nimes aqueduct is a masterpiece.

Other remnants of Roman influence are sprinkled throughout Europe and the Mediterranean region. Many roadways that are used today follow routes laid out and paved by Roman workers. The extensive network of Roman roads held the empire together at the height of its power. Some Roman bridges are still in use too, proof of the skill that built them 2,000 years ago. The Roman Empire is gone, but its legacy remains. It is literally written in stone.

A Visit with Dolphins

by Amy Hall

Latin Roots *aqua, dict*

aquatic   dictionary   predicted

Mace had been looking forward to the trip on a dolphin-watching boat for a long time. Grandpa had predicted they would have a great time, and Mace was certain he would be right.

As they boarded the boat, passengers were handed orange life vests to wear. Mace put his on and sat down next to Grandpa.

Soon the boat moved away from the pier. One of the boat operators told the passengers some facts about dolphins and other aquatic creatures they might see during the trip.

When they were a few miles out, the boat slowed and stopped. It gently bobbed up and down in the waves. A few moments later, the first silvery fin appeared, followed by another, and then another. Mace stood up to get a better look. Then a dolphin leaped. Mace lost his balance. At the same moment, a large wave made the boat rock hard. Mace landed in the water.

The life vest kept Mace afloat, but it couldn't keep him from panicking. The crew of the boat sprung into action, tossing him a rope with a ring attached to it to pull him back in. Mace tried to get hold of the ring. Then he saw a silver snout poke through the ring, and a pair of kind, intelligent eyes looked at him. A dolphin had come to the rescue! Mace was too amazed to be scared anymore. The beautiful creature pushed the ring within Mace's reach, then disappeared. Mace was soon back in the boat, wrapped in a blanket and staring out where his aquatic friend was leaping in the waves. There are no words in the dictionary to describe how he felt at that moment.

Suddenly Mace heard a bell ringing and he woke up. It had just been a dream. Now it was time to get up and get ready to go to the pier with Grandpa.

Brilliant Ben Franklin

by Karen Stine

Prefixes *im-* and *in-*

immortal	independence	inefficient
impossible	independent	inexhaustible
inadequate	indisputably	injustice

17

It would be hard to describe American colonial society, and impossible to describe the birth of the United States, without talking about Benjamin Franklin. He was one of the most famous and politically active founders of the nation. He was also a popular writer, a brilliant scientist, a busy inventor, and a man who actively sought to improve society for all citizens.

Franklin only went to school until he was about ten years old. Still, his sharp mind, love of reading, and desire to understand the world gave him the best education. At age twelve, he went to work for his brother James in order to learn to be a printer. In 1723, at the age of only seventeen, he moved from Boston to Philadelphia, and then from Philadelphia to England, to learn more about printing. When he returned to Philadelphia in 1726, he set up his own print shop. He was very successful and became quite wealthy.

Franklin organized a club in Philadelphia that met to discuss politics and culture. It was with club members that Franklin discussed ideas for social improvements. For example, he saw that there was no system for fighting fires in the city. He proposed the development of a fire department. He also thought that the few night watchmen were inadequate for a city the size of Philadelphia. This led to the establishment of a city police force. His inexhaustible supply of creativity brought about other community services as well. He started a library, a hospital, an insurance company, and an academy that would eventually become the University of Pennsylvania.

Franklin was also drawn to the new science of electricity. He studied new inventions and read everything he could find on the subject. He also did his own experiments. One of his friends published Franklin's writings about electricity. The book became a big hit. Other scientists used Franklin's book to learn basics of electricity.

Franklin's cleverness showed in other ways too. He was an avid inventor. He saw that relying on the fireplace for heat was inefficient and uncomfortable, so he invented a new kind of heating stove. The Franklin stove became a regular feature in people's homes for almost 200 years. He invented the lightning rod to save homes and other buildings from lightning strikes. This simple device attracted lightning during a storm and drew the electricity safely to the ground. He invented special eyeglasses called bifocals. He created a type of musical instrument called a glass harmonica. He made swim fins to make swimming easier. He invented the odometer—a device to measure how far a vehicle had traveled. His ideas seemed endless!

Among Benjamin Franklin's many inventions were bifocals for seeing both up close and at a distance.

Franklin loved Britain. He spent almost twenty years of his life there. He considered himself a royalist, or a supporter of the king. Franklin thought it was best that the American colonies remain part of Great Britain. However, he began to see the injustice of the system. He tried to bring about changes that would be fairer, but eventually he joined those American leaders who sought freedom from Great Britain.

The part for which Franklin is most remembered is indisputably his leading role in writing the Declaration of Independence. He was one of the chief figures in the effort to make the American colonies an independent nation.

Benjamin Franklin died in 1790 at the age of 84. Yet his accomplishments, inventions, and public service live on today. This great man's ideas are truly immortal.

Clean Water for All

by Wendy Mobley

Prefixes _im-_ and _in-_

impossible	inadequate	insufficient
impure	inefficient	invariably

Some researchers estimate that almost a billion people today live in places where it is hard or impossible to get clean water. Millions get sick and die from diseases that they get through impure water. Inadequate sanitation, inefficient plumbing, and a lack of education add to the problem. Waste and garbage are clogging people's sources of water. Invariably, the people most likely to suffer in this situation are those who already live in deep poverty.

There are many organizations that have an interest in improving clean water access. They target places and people with insufficient means to make improvements themselves. Some of this work focuses on digging new wells and cleaning up old ones in high-risk areas. Others focus on building up sanitation systems and teaching people to protect their water sources. Still others focus on providing efficient filters for families so they can safely use the water available to them.

Volunteers can get involved in a number of ways. They can take time to learn more about the issue of clean water access. They can write letters to their representatives in the government to urge them to take an active interest in the problem. They can organize or attend fundraisers to help pay for clean water projects. Some people even go to places where they can help community members dig wells and clean waterways.

It can be overwhelming to think about how to improve conditions for a billion people. But the best solutions start small. Change happens one village at a time, one well at a time.

Minding Your Ps and Qs

by Jim Guenther

Prefixes *im-* and *in-*

impolite   incapable   inconsiderate

improper

Have you ever heard someone say to "mind your Ps and Qs"? They were saying, "Be on your best behavior." They were talking about something called etiquette.

Etiquette is learning and using behaviors that are considered polite. In the past, children sometimes had etiquette classes at school or in the community. These included lessons on polite speech. Children even learned that there were proper and improper ways of eating at the table. Of course, they were expected to follow the proper ways!

Rules about etiquette can be complicated. Etiquette books have been written as guides. If you saw one of these books, you might feel completely incapable of actually doing anything right! But there are simple things that everyone can remember to avoid being impolite.

One thing to remember is that simple kindness goes a long way. Greeting someone nicely will make him or her feel more comfortable, and remembering to say "please" and "thank you" will make people more likely to help you.

Also think about other people when you decide to do something. For example, it is seen as inconsiderate to take a seat on a bus if an older person is still standing. It is also impolite to listen to loud music or talk loudly on your phone in a public place. Think about how your choices affect people around you.

The "Golden Rule" is still the best rule to remember when it comes to etiquette. Treat other people how you want them to treat you. If you remember that, you probably won't need etiquette classes or books. You'll be doing it naturally!

The Transatlantic Telegraph

by Tammy Flores

The ship *Great Eastern* failed in its first attempt to lay cable for the transatlantic telegraph but later succeeded.

Greek and Latin Prefixes *trans-*, *tele-*

telegraph	transformed	transport
transatlantic	transoceanic	

When the electric telegraph was put into wider use in the 1830s, it transformed communication dramatically. Before, a written message had to be carried across land and sea. It could take days, weeks, or even months for news to get from one place to another. With the electric telegraph, messages could be carried from point to point in seconds. The problem was that each of those points had to be connected by wires. Often, telegraph companies would set up their wires along the railroad routes. As the railroads expanded, more and more cities were connected. By the 1850s, more than 20,000 miles of telegraph wire were connecting cities and towns across the United States.

That system worked really well . . . for reaching people across land. However, getting messages across large bodies of water was still a problem. News between Europe and the Americas had to travel by ship. In 1840, that journey could take more than three weeks. Even when faster steamships were making the journey, the fastest ships took about 12 days. In 1850, the first effort was made to get wires across the English Channel to connect England and France. The cables had to go underwater for a distance of about 20 miles. The wires had to be insulated very well in order to stand up to the pressure of all the water above them. The first underwater cable didn't work well, and it had to be repaired. Repairing an underwater cable was a huge challenge!

Only a few years later, several attempts were made to lay a transatlantic underwater telegraph cable from Ireland to Newfoundland. That was more than 2,000 miles! It took four ships and five attempts to finish those 2,000 miles. On August 5, 1858, that first cable was connected and put into use. On August 16, U.S. President James Buchanan and Britain's Queen Victoria exchanged polite messages by telegraph. Unfortunately, the insulation on this cable was not good enough to protect the telegraph wires from the ocean water, and it stopped working in September.

Cyrus W. Field worked to make sure cables for the telegraph could cross the ocean and connect North America with Europe.

The dream of a transatlantic telegraph did not die with that first attempt. An American businessman named Cyrus W. Field was determined to see this accomplished. The cables were improved so they would last longer. An enormous ship, the *Great Eastern*, was designed specifically to transport the huge coils of cable that were required for the effort. In 1865, the *Great Eastern* set sail to begin the difficult job. The first journey failed when the cable snapped and was lost. In 1866, another attempt was made. This time, workers not only succeeded in laying one cable, but they found the cable that had broken on the first journey, repaired it, and finished that line as well. Telegraph engineers worked quickly to get the system connected, and it worked perfectly. This journey was a complete success. Soon, other transoceanic cables were being laid. The world instantly became a much smaller place. News from around the world could be heard in American cities in a matter of moments, rather than months.

A Mission for Mother's Day

by Seth Villon

Greek and Latin Prefixes *trans-, tele-*

telephone	translate	transportation
television	transmit	transported
transformed		

"We have a big chance for you to do something really special for your mom this Mother's Day," said the television news announcer. "You could win an all-day pampering spa package for your mother, complete with transportation and dinner for two. All you have to do is write an essay of 500 words or less, telling us why your mother is the best."

Mark *knew* his mom was the best mom in the world, but would he be able to translate what he felt into words that could convince the television station? The instructions had said 500 words or less. What if he didn't use any words at all? Mark decided to use photographs to transmit his ideas. After all, he thought, they say "a picture is worth a thousand words."

29

Mark looked through the family photo albums to find pictures, and he selected one for each year of his life. One photograph showed her on the floor with him, holding a toy telephone for him to play with. Another showed her holding both of his hands while he was taking his first wobbly steps. Another showed her standing behind him with her arms around him, showing him how to hold a baseball bat correctly. Another showed her sitting on the couch with him, reading a book.

Mark scanned each photo and put them into a document, and then he wrote a short description of each. Finally, he added one last thought: "My mom has been there for me every day of my life. She has taught me, cheered me, taken care of me, transported me, and transformed me. She is definitely the best mom in the world."

He made two copies of the essay, one to mail to the television station and the other to give to his mom on Mother's Day. That way, even if they didn't win, she would still know—at least a little—what a great mom she was.

Inventions That Transformed the World

by Zeva Schiffer

Greek and Latin Prefixes *trans-*, *tele-*

telephone(s)   transform(ed)   transportation

Can you imagine living life today without a telephone? What would life be like without computers and cars? A hundred years ago, most people didn't know much about any of these things. These inventions have transformed the way we live our daily lives so much that it would be hard to do without them!

The first telephone was tested successfully in 1876. Since then, many improvements have been made. Satellites and wireless technology made cell phones possible. Researchers expect that by 2014 there will be more cell phones in use than there are people on the planet! Telephones are our number one way of staying in touch.

Computers have also transformed our world. The first personal computer (a computer that was meant to be operated by one person using a keyboard) was made available for sale in 1957. Since then, computers have become smaller, faster, more powerful, and less expensive. Many tablet computers fit in the palm of your hand. Computer technology is used to run many things: cars, planes, medical equipment, and even coffeemakers and vacuum cleaners!

The area of transportation has seen some of the most dramatic changes. The idea of a vehicle that could move by its own power had been a dream for a long time. In 1885 the first gasoline-powered cars were made in Germany. As cars improved and became cheaper, more and more people bought them. In 2004, there were more than 240 million cars and trucks registered in the United States alone!

These three inventions have changed the way we live. Imagine what today's inventions will do to transform the world of tomorrow!

Greek Theater

by Keith Moss

This amphitheater built around A.D. 160 in ancient Athens is still used today.

Greek Prefixes *amphi-*, *anti-*

amphitheater(s)   anticlimax   antithesis

Have you ever been to a play at the theater? If so, you have the ancient Greeks to thank for it. Theater-going was a very important part of the culture of ancient Greece. Other cultures had drama, too, but the Greeks seemed to be the first that had theater productions on such a huge scale. Greek cities held contests for the best plays and playwrights. They bragged to one another about the quality of their cities' plays. It was a matter of great honor to have a great playwright in your city.

Greek drama was a bit different from the types of plays you have probably seen. In Greek theater, the actors didn't usually speak. Instead, they wore masks and acted out the scenes. A chorus stood in front of the stage and told the story. In order to be seen and understood by people all over the theater, the actors used very dramatic body movements. The masks, too, were large and exaggerated. That way, people in the very back would be able to tell if the character was happy, sad, and so on. You may have seen a picture of two masks that are used to stand for drama or theater. One is very sad looking and one very happy. That symbol is based on the masks that Greek actors wore.

Most plays in ancient Greece told about Greek mythology. The audience often was already familiar with the story. However, audience members were eager to see how each playwright would tell the story in a new way. Plays were one of three types. *Tragedy* plays always had a hero who faced terrible circumstances and losses.

Usually, the hero had what is called a tragic flaw. That is a trait, such as pride, that caused his problem. Tragedies were written and performed to help the audience think about how to live better. The antithesis of this was the *comedy* play. In Greek comedies, the story always had a happy ending for the hero. That didn't mean that it was always funny in the way we think of comedy today. If you wanted to see something funny, you would have seen a *satyr* play. (That's the origin of the English word *satire*, which means using humor to show and criticize the silliness of another person.) Satyr plays were often performed between acts of a play to poke fun at some of the serious themes in a tragedy.

THEATRE OF DIONYSOS AT ATHENS.

Every town had at least one amphitheater. Amphitheaters were among the largest buildings in a town. They were oval and often built on a hillside. There was a small building and stage in front and rows of seats encircling them on the slope of the hill. They were designed to seat thousands of people. Amphitheaters were open, without roofs, which meant theater productions only took place in daytime and in fine weather. Fortunately, Greece is a very sunny place! There were no microphones or speakers. Instead, these buildings were designed in a way that helped the speakers' voices to be heard all over the building.

We even have the Greeks to thank for many of the words used in performing arts. *Thespians* (that's a fancy name for actors), *scene, climax* and *anticlimax, orchestra, chorus, drama, tragedy, comedy,* and even *theater* all have Greek origins. So the next time someone tells you about a play or movie, you can smile and tell them, "It's all Greek to me!"

Fantastic Frogs

by Becca Sanger

Greek Prefixes *amphi-*, *anti-*

amphibians	antibacterial	antifreeze
amphibious	antidote	antiseptic

Frogs are some of the most common animals in the world. They can be found in every region except Antarctica. Different species can survive in temperatures ranging from the blazing heat of deserts to the frozen Arctic areas.

Frogs belong to a class of animals called amphibians. These are animals that can live both in water and on land. This adaptability is part of what has helped frogs stay in existence for millions of years. If there is danger on land, a frog can hop into the water. If there is a shortage of food underwater, a frog can hop out in search of food on land. Amphibians like to keep their options open! Other amphibious animals include toads, salamanders, and newts.

Frogs have many traits that help them survive extremes. Frogs that live in desert areas burrow deep into the earth or mud and create protective cocoons. This helps their skin stay moist when the water is gone. Frogs in Arctic areas also burrow deep down and go into a type of hibernation. Their blood pools in their vital organs. It acts like a kind of antifreeze until it is warm enough for the frog to start moving again.

About 200 species of frogs have poisonous skins. The poisons are strong enough that you would need to have an antidote on hand. Fortunately, these frogs are very easy to spot because of their bright colors. These poisonous frogs are dangerous, but they may be able to do a lot of good too. Scientists have found that some of these frog poisons can help stop pain, and others can block infections because of their antiseptic, antibacterial properties. That's big work for such a small animal!

A Day at the Colosseum

by Trish Amato

Greek Prefixes *amphi-*, *anti-*

amphitheater   antidote   antisocial

anticlimax

Claudius ran along the stone-paved street. His father said that they would go to see the chariot races today if he finished his chores. It would be his first time to go! Claudius ran to the market to get the vegetables his mother wanted, and he stopped at the leatherworker's shop to get a new thong for his sandals. Then he ran the whole way home.

His father smiled as he ran in breathless. His father knew that the promise of a trip to the new arena would help Claudius get his tasks done quickly. It was a good antidote for his usual slowness. They grabbed some small loaves of bread for a snack, threw their short cloaks over their shoulders, and left.

Many people were out in the streets this afternoon, and most of them were headed to the races. Claudius saw his friend Maximus walking with his brother and hoped they would find seats near one another.

As they drew near the Colosseum, Claudius was in awe. The walls were enormous, and they seemed to stretch up to the sky. They joined the crowds entering through the many gates. Claudius had never been in such a huge place. The Colosseum was an amphitheater, a roofless, oval building with seating for 45,000 people. There was no way to be antisocial in such a place! It seemed today that all 45,000 seats were filled, and everyone was excited and chatty, waiting for the excitement to begin.

Soon, the races got underway. Claudius was amazed by the speed and daring of the drivers. The show was the best he had ever seen. In comparison, the music performance—by a very famous singer—that followed was an anticlimax. Claudius couldn't wait until the next time he could come to the Colosseum.

A Ride Back in Time

by Ben Cleveland

Passengers wait to board a train pulled by a steam engine in the early 1900s.

Synonyms and Antonyms

antique, old/new	historic/modern	less/more
closed/open		loudly, noisily/silently
common/special, unusual		

Old Clem was a historic landmark in the county. Clem had been silently parked in the old train switching yard at the edge of town for more years than most people could remember. Then Mr. Lemmons, a local historian, made a proposal to the town council. He wanted to restore Old Clem to its former glory as the finest steam locomotive that had ever run on the rails.

Old Clem had been built in 1920. It had pulled train cars filled with coal, grain, cattle, cargo, and passengers from one end of the state to the other for more than thirty years. As electric engines and car and truck transportation became more common, Old Clem had been used less and less. In 1952 it was finally put out of service. Still, Old Clem was well loved by the people of Pine Grove. They left it in the train yard as a reminder of simpler times.

When the town council announced that Old Clem was to run again, the local businesses were quite enthusiastic. They gave money and supplies to help with the project. Mr. Lemmon found an expert who knew all about steam engines. They worked together to replace and repair broken, rusty parts. It was almost two years before Old Clem was ready to run again.

In the meantime, Mr. Lemmons also worked on getting the passenger carriages cleaned and repaired. He found antique light fixtures to replace those that were missing. He repaired the broken springs in the old seats and carefully patched and mended the velvet curtains.

He cleaned everything so that it shined and sparkled like new.

Finally, the day arrived when Old Clem would make its first journey in sixty years. The tickets for this trip had sold out in just an hour. Many people wanted to experience a ride on this antique train! Everyone who came on board admired the beautiful job Mr. Lemmons had done. They felt as though they had stepped out of the modern world and into the year 1920! Mr. Lemmons was on board for this special trip as the conductor. He collected tickets from the excited passengers and showed them to their seats.

Many people traveled long distances aboard trains in the early 1900s.

When the passenger cars were full and the doors were closed, the station master blew the station's whistle loudly. Mr. Lemmons clanged a bell in answer. The engineer blew a blast on Old Clem's whistle. Then the steam began to puff out, and the train slowly pulled out of the station. For half an hour, Old Clem chugged and puffed noisily. Steam and smoke drifted back over the train. Some of it came into the passenger cars through the open windows. However, the passengers were too fascinated by this unusual journey to mind. A microphone and speaker system had been set up on board for this special occasion. While the train rattled along, Mr. Lemmons shared the history of locomotives and told stories about train travel in the past.

It felt as though no time at all had passed before Old Clem pulled the train into the station again. As all the passengers got off, they talked happily about the journey. Many hoped for another chance in the future to ride the historic train. Old Clem was going to be busy for a long time giving a new generation a taste of old times.

Tornadoes

by Susan Lee

Synonyms and Antonyms

cool/warm

damaging, destructive

dangerous/ safe

dry/moist

enormous, large/ small

strong/weak

Tornadoes are one of the most destructive types of weather. A tornado is a rotating column of air that usually forms from a thunderstorm cloud. Some are quite weak. They might blow trashcans over, tear off small tree branches, and take shingles off houses. But other tornadoes can be quite strong. The damaging winds can reach speeds of 300 miles per hour. These dangerous storms have the ability to pick up cars and houses, uproot large trees, and carry things many miles away. Every year more than a thousand tornadoes are reported in the United States, and some of those tornadoes cause millions of dollars' worth of damage.

Most tornadoes form when a mass of warm, moist air and a mass of cool, dry air meet in the atmosphere. This causes instability and rapid changes in wind direction and speed. Enormous thunderclouds develop. As these clouds begin to move and rotate, funnel clouds form. When a funnel cloud stretches all the way to the ground, it is called a tornado.

Tornadoes can occur anywhere and at any time of year, but there are times when these storms are more common. In the southern U.S. states, tornadoes are more common in March, April, and May. In northern areas, tornado season is more often in the summer. Weather scientists have a system they use to warn people. When a tornado is possible but not certain, a tornado watch is issued. When tornadoes have actually been sighted nearby, a tornado warning is issued. Television and radio stations help pass these warnings on to the public. Pay attention to these warnings and get to a safe place in your home if you hear them!

A Comet Tale

by Nancy Whelan

Synonyms and Antonyms

amazing, spectacular

ancient/modern

grows, stretches/ shrinks

important, serious

irregular/regular

large/small, tiny

occasionally, sometimes

Edmund Halley was reading about comets, and he noticed an interesting pattern. Comets are balls of frozen water, gases, and rock particles. They travel in regular orbits. Halley thought that large comets reported in 1531, 1607, and 1682 were actually the same comet. He predicted that it would next appear in 1758, and it did! The comet is called Halley's Comet in Edmund Halley's honor.

Halley's Comet orbits the sun. It comes close enough to be seen on Earth on average every 76 years. (It is actually slightly irregular, because other objects in the solar system affect its orbit.) It is quite large, as comets go, though much too small to be a planet. Halley's Comet has a tail of gases, water vapor, and tiny rock particles. This tail shrinks and grows, depending on where the comet is in its orbit. Sometimes it stretches for millions of miles in space. Occasionally, our planet passes through this tail. The particles then cause lovely meteor showers.

Halley's Comet can be quite spectacular to watch. In ancient times, people saw this amazing comet, and they were frightened. They believed it meant something very serious and important was about to happen. Now modern scientists have seen and studied Halley's Comet. They understand a lot about it. Still it remains an incredible sight. Halley's Comet last appeared in 1986. It is scheduled to make its next appearance in 2061.

The Eskimo Way of Life

by Ryan Fischer

Words from French

caribou	excellent	raged
captured	extreme	region
community	fruits	supplies
descendants	patiently	survive
entire	periods	traditional

The snowstorm had raged off and on during the whole three days of their hunt. They had tracked a herd of caribou. Now hunters waited patiently and silently for a clear shot. A few moments later, three of the mighty caribou were captured. This successful hunt would help the family survive through the long, harsh winter. This was life for the Eskimo people.

Eskimos are members of related groups of people indigenous to cold Arctic areas. Eskimo groups live in Alaska, Canada, and Greenland. They speak dialects, or related forms, of the Inuit language. Their lifestyles are well adapted to the extreme cold and ice of the Arctic region.

Because Eskimos live in places where most plants, including fruits and vegetables, cannot grow, traditional diets were heavily made up of meats, fat, and fish. The people hunted seals, whales, caribou, and elk. Almost all of the parts of these animals were put to use. Eskimos were also skilled fishers.

Good protective clothing is absolutely vital in such a harsh climate as that of the Arctic. Caribou skins made lightweight but very warm parkas. Caribou fur was worn during the coldest periods of winter. Pelts from other animals would be used to make light parkas. These were handy during the breezy, cool summer season. Waterproof parkas made from whale intestine might be worn over fur parkas. This would protect the people from seawater during whaling trips. Feathered bird hides also held in heat well. Eskimos made colorful, festive coats with the hides and feathers. Boots, gloves, boat coverings, and tents were also made from the hides of hunted animals. The women had the task of sewing clothes and coverings. It was a big job to keep the entire community protected against the ice, snow, and cold. Now Eskimo descendants also wear store-bought clothes, coats, and boots.

This family is building an igloo from ice blocks.

Traditionally, Eskimo people who lived inland would have houses constructed from thick blocks of ice and snow. These houses were called igloos. In coastal areas, Eskimo people usually created sod and earthen houses that were supported with wood or whalebone frames. These homes were very well insulated and could be quite warm. In the warmer summer months, tents of animal skins were also used.

Eskimo people learned to use almost anything they were able to find in their environment. Driftwood was used to make hunting arrows, dolls, bowls, and tools. Ivory from frozen and fossilized mastodons could be turned into very fine, sharp needles, knives, scrapers, and other tools. Whalebone made good building supplies for homes and boats. Fish skins were found to make excellent waterproof baskets.

Dogsleds were the most important means of land transportation. Kayaks, or covered one-person canoes, were used for fishing on the rivers or hunting for seals. Larger, raft-like boats were used for whale hunting. Now snowmobiles and modern boats with outboard motors are replacing these traditional modes of transportation.

Traditional ways of life based on hunting, fishing, and trading are quickly disappearing. Many Eskimo people have moved into towns and have taken jobs in mining and oil drilling. Still, some Eskimo traditions are being preserved.

The Family Restaurant

by Eliza Lewis

Words from French

apartment	dinner	restaurant
chef's	menu(s)	routine
cover	parents	scenes
customer(s)	pencils	table

Teresa sat in the booth and finished her homework, just as she did every afternoon. Almost every day for her family began and ended in this restaurant. The family lived in a large apartment upstairs, but most of their family life took place in the restaurant. Before Teresa awoke in the morning, her parents were downstairs opening up and serving the early-morning customers. She and her brothers always ate breakfast at the family table in the back corner. After school, they came back and worked on homework before having dinner at the same corner table. This had been the family routine for as long as Teresa could remember.

When they were old enough, Teresa's brothers had begun to help out in the restaurant during the dinner rush. Teresa wanted to help too, but her mom said she was too young. She sat alone at the family table or went upstairs to read in her room. Sometimes she brought her pad and pencils down and practiced her drawing, often choosing scenes in the restaurant as subjects.

One day a customer walked by and saw her art. It was a picture of her dad in his chef's hat.

"Why, that looks just like him!" the woman declared. She asked if Teresa would draw a picture for her. Soon a small group was waiting around Teresa's table as she created pictures for each person. Her mom watched while this was going on and began to form a plan for getting Teresa more involved with the restaurant.

That evening, Teresa's mother asked her to draw a new cover for the menu. Teresa was so thrilled that she got to work right away, and soon a cheerful new cover was ready to be printed. Teresa beamed as she helped her mom hand out the menus to customers, feeling like she was finally part of the family business.

The Little Houses of Laura Ingalls Wilder

by Tom Tourneau

Words from French		
articles	encouraged	memories
cabin	frontier	prairie
courage	magazines	rural

Laura Ingalls Wilder started life in a little cabin in rural Wisconsin. When she was born in 1867, the Midwest was still considered a frontier. Land was cheap, but it took a lot of courage and energy to live life there. Laura and her family moved many times during her childhood. Her father was trying to find a way to earn a living and make a lasting home for his family.

Because they moved so much, Laura and her sisters learned mostly at home. This helped Laura realize how important education was. At the age of 15, she became a teacher in a rural school. She also loved to write, so she sent articles to magazines and newspapers.

Laura told her children many stories of her childhood on the frontier. She had very happy memories of the many different places where her family had lived. She also remembered the historical changes that took place during the time. Later, Laura's daughter Rose encouraged her to write these stories so others could enjoy them.

Laura Ingalls Wilder published her first book, *Little House in the Big Woods*, in 1932. It told about her family's life in that Wisconsin cabin. Other books followed. *Little House on the Prairie* told about life on a South Dakota homestead. *On the Banks of Plum Creek*, *By the Shores of Silver Lake*, *The Long Winter*, *Little Town on the Prairie*, and *These Happy Golden Years* told about other places and experiences in Laura's life. These books became very popular. Many children got a glimpse of frontier life through Wilder's writing.

Clowning Around

by Wanda Washington

Suffixes -ous, -able, -ible

bulbous	generous	permissible
capable	humorous	possible
enormous	impossible	recognizable
famous	lovable	ridiculous
flexible	memorable	spontaneous

Perhaps you've seen them at circuses, parties, or parades. With their painted faces, funny clothes, and humorous antics, clowns have long been a part of our entertainment.

The first professional clowns appeared in Greek and Roman plays. They sometimes came on stage to make fun of the characters in a story. Sometimes they were the object of other characters' jokes. Later, court jesters were common in the halls of kings, queens, and other rulers. It was rarely permissible to laugh at a ruler, but occasionally the jester could get away with it. Usually it was safer for these jokers to direct their humor at someone other than a grumpy monarch!

57

Clowns similar to those we see today traveled with acting troupes that went from town to town in the Middle Ages. Like modern clowns, they wore baggy clothes and big shoes. They painted their faces and did exaggerated, foolish things to make the audience laugh.

The first circus clown was an Englishman named Joseph Grimaldi. He used what is called physical comedy. His tripping, falling, and bumping into things and people got lots of laughs. Clowns are often called "joeys" in honor of this famous clown.

Clowns still perform with traveling circuses around the world.

The Tramp was a character Charlie Chaplin made famous in some of his earliest movies.

The easily recognizable costume of most clowns has been almost unchanged for two hundred years: ridiculous coats and ruffles, enormous shoes, and silly hats. Faces are commonly painted white with exaggerated, colorful features. A big, bulbous nose is a common part of the costume.

Clowns usually have to be pretty talented. In fact, there are clowning schools and "colleges" where many modern-day clowns go to learn their skills. Clowns are capable of making seemingly impossible activities look easy and goofy. For example, one clown gag is to fit a dozen or more clowns into a tiny car. Some clowns make balloon animals. Some do imitations or juggle. All clowns learn to be spontaneous, flexible, and—above all—funny.

There have been many lovable, memorable clowns. Charlie Chaplin became famous as a clown performer in early movies. Emmett Kelly was a "vagabond clown" who traveled around the United States performing in circuses and shows for many years. Red Skelton was a performer from the time he was ten years old. He had very successful radio and television programs in which he clowned around.

Clowning isn't just about fun and games. Many clowning organizations have generous members who give their time and clowning skills to raise money for good causes. Others visit children and adults who are in the hospital. According to the clowns and the patients, laughter really is very good medicine. Patch Adams is an American clown who also happens to be a real-life doctor. He started an organization called Gesundheit! Institute. (*Gesundheit* is a German word people often say to one another when they sneeze. It means "good health.") One purpose is to help people see the health benefits of being happy and positive. Patch teaches doctors to use humor and fun. He also organizes humanitarian clown work. Clown groups go around the world to visit orphanages, nursing homes, hospitals, schools, and public parks in poor places. The joy that clowning brings makes it possible to change the world!

The Cliff Dwellers

by David Lin

Suffixes -ous, -able, -ible

desirable	mysterious	terrible
incredible	possible	unreachable
marvelous	precious	wondrous

Hidden in a canyon and rising up several stories under the overhang of a cliff is a mysterious sight. It is the home of a community that disappeared 700 years ago. The Anasazi, who are ancestors of the modern Pueblo people of the American Southwest, built their homes against these cliffs. They used the natural rock formations and their own incredible skill with stonework and adobe (a type of clay) to create marvelous homes and villages.

61

These wondrous examples of ancient architecture are found mostly in the Four Corners area. That is where Arizona, Utah, New Mexico, and Colorado meet. Some cliff dwellings were four or five stories high. Often, the upper floors were set back a little from the levels below. This way, the roof of one floor could serve as a terrace or balcony for the one above. The ground floor was reached by climbing up to the roof on a ladder and then down through the ceiling. Upper floors were reached by other doors and ladders. In times of danger, the ladders would be pulled up. Then even the ground floor was unreachable.

The Anasazi people probably raised crops on the plateaus above them or in the canyons below. They also sent out hunting parties to bring back food. No one is quite certain why the cliff dwellings were suddenly abandoned around 1300. It is possible that a terrible drought wiped out crops and sources of drinking water. If so, the Anasazi may have been forced to move on to a more desirable location. They would have gone in search of the precious, life-giving resource of water.

At the Farmers' Market

by Kelly Dillard

Suffixes -ous, -able, -ible

affordable	famous	portable
delicious	generous	scrumptious
edible	nutritious	

Madison and Jacob had stayed with their aunt and uncle before. They owned an old farm where they raised chickens for eggs. Usually, Uncle Jim drove into town every Saturday with all the eggs they had gathered. He sold them at the weekly farmers' market. Today, Uncle Jim and Aunt May decided to make it a family trip. Madison and Jacob hopped in the seat behind Jim and May and rode to town.

The farmers' market was bigger and more colorful than they had imagined. Jim set up the portable booth where he sold the eggs. May walked with the twins to show them the market. Everywhere they looked they saw fresh, nutritious foods. One farmer had piles of edible mushrooms that smelled very earthy. Another had baskets of scrumptious berries in bright colors. One generous apple farmer gave them cups with fresh, fragrant apple juice. A dairy farmer gave them samples of delicious cheese.

May took them to a booth where her friend Carol sold her famous blueberry muffins. They each got one to enjoy. Then they shopped all over the market to find the most affordable produce. They passed soap and candle makers, honey sellers, flower stands, seed sellers, and basket makers. They listened to a musician who played folk songs.

Before long, Jim had sold all the eggs and packed up the booth. The kids were worn out and ready to go home. They had never imagined that there could be so much to see and do at the market!

The Tryout

by Ann Marie Trefny

Related Words

active/activity

announced/ announcement

audience/ audition/ auditorium

beautiful/ beautifully

calm/calmly

certain/ certainly

confidence/ confident/ confidently

encourage(d)/ encouragement/ encouraging

energetic/energy

hard/harder

memorized/ memory/remember

music/musical/ musician

nerves/nervous/ nervously

peaceful/ peacefully

perfect/perfectly

perform/ performance/ performing

rehearsal(s)/ rehearsed

relax/ relaxation

sang/sing/ singer/singing/ song(s)/sung

select/ selecting/ selections

slow/slowly

Quinn had always loved singing. In the shower, in his room, in the car, walking down the street, this musical boy always had a song ready to sing. So, when he heard the announcement that the community arts center was forming a children's choir, he knew this was the perfect activity for him and that he had to try out.

The flier that announced the tryouts said all interested children should prepare three selections to sing for the audition. Quinn spent a lot of time selecting just the right music. He wanted it to be beautiful, but he also knew he had to select something that would show his skill and personality best. Quinn chose one song that he had sung in the school musical the previous year. Another one was a peaceful lullaby that he learned from his mother. The third was a folk song that was fun, active, and energetic—just like the singer himself!

Quinn rehearsed for an hour every day. He tried to sing the fun songs with a lot of energy and the quiet song peacefully. He knew that being able to control the mood was important for a singer. Quinn also memorized the songs so that he knew them by heart. Sometimes he stumbled over the words or missed a note, but then he would just practice harder. His last rehearsal went perfectly, without a single flaw. Finally, the day of the tryouts came.

Quinn arrived at the audition with his mom and his sister Mikala. They followed the signs to the area near the auditorium where all the children were waiting. They all were looking nervously around. Quinn realized he too was nervous. He certainly hadn't expected that! After all, he loved singing and music. He had spent hours practicing and had committed these songs to memory. He thought he would calm himself by going over the words again one more time. Then, horrified, he realized he couldn't remember the words anymore!

Quinn's older sister Mikala was a musician, so she knew all about nerves before a performance. She had expected Quinn to feel nervous and came to encourage him. She found him in the waiting area, where he was trying to remember the words that had slipped his mind. Mikala led him to a sofa to sit down. She encouraged him to slow down his breathing as she got him a glass of water. As he slowly drank it, she told him how important it was to relax, just as she did before performing, so that he could perform well. Mikala's encouragement helped him calm down, and her encouraging words reminded him that he could really do this after all of his practice. With that relaxation, Quinn became confident that he could remember the words again.

When his name was called, Quinn calmly took his place on stage. The music began, and he sang his songs beautifully and with confidence, even better than in rehearsals. Mikala met him backstage with a huge hug and a grin that boosted his confidence even more. He was certain he would make it in the choir. He was also certain that he could sing confidently in front of any audience if he continued to work hard and believe in himself.

Unraveling the Hieroglyphic Mystery

by Curt Pinney

Related Words

discovered/discovery

Egypt/Egyptian

French/Frenchman

hieroglyphs/hieroglyphic(s)

mysterious/mystery

scholars/scholarly

theorize/theory

translate/translating/translation/untranslated

When archeologists entered the great pyramids of Egypt to see the treasures of the past, one thing they found in abundance were pictures. Rows and rows of mysterious pictures carved and painted on the walls, tombs, and plaques. These pictures seemed to tell a story, but few people who were still alive could read that story any more. These pictures were hieroglyphics, a special form of writing used by ancient Egyptian priests.

Experts studied these markings for many years to try to make sense of them. Some markings seemed to stand for the names of gods and kings. This led scholars to theorize that the pictures were telling a story, somewhat like an ancient comic book. Another scholarly theory suggested that the symbols stood for words or word parts. That still didn't help with the translation of the symbols. There were more than 700 symbols and no way to match them to individual sounds or words. The mystery of Egyptian hieroglyphics remained unsolved.

It wasn't until 1799 that the key to this mystery was discovered. A group of French soldiers found a broken stone that appeared to have three different languages carved on it. It turned out to be a message that had been written in Greek, hieroglyphics, and demotic script. That was a form of writing that was used more commonly in Egypt. The discovery of this stone, known as the Rosetta Stone, helped scholars to finally translate some of the hieroglyphs. Still, most remained untranslated for another 20 years.

In 1822, after years of hard work, a Frenchman named Jean-Francois Champollion had a breakthrough. He was able to unravel the mystery and open up a whole new world of study. Scholars began translating and seeking to understand the stories the ancient Egyptians left behind.

MyPlate for Good Health

by Adele Klinkner

Related Words

choice(s)/choosing

confusing/confusion

eat/eating

freezer/frozen

health/healthful/
healthfully/
healthy

nutrients/
nutrition/
nutritious

simple/simply

You can find lots of rules about what to eat and what not to eat. Getting good nutrition can be a bit confusing. To help people of all ages make the most nutritious choices with the least confusion, the U.S. Department of Agriculture created MyPlate in 2011. This simple guide helps people know what combinations of foods will give them the most healthful mix of nutrients.

The idea can be summed up simply. When you eat, your plate should be half-filled with fruits and vegetables. One quarter should be lean protein. Another quarter should be healthy grains. A low-fat dairy choice such as a small glass of reduced-fat milk will round out a healthy meal. You can look at the USDA Web site to find ideas for healthy snacks and meals to maintain good health. There you will find lots of fun and easy tips for choosing nutritious foods. You can also find activities that will get you moving and having fun.

Here are a few ideas to make eating healthfully more fun.

- Dip it! Use a fruit-flavored low-fat yogurt as a dip for apple slices. Or add some herbs to plain yogurt to make a tasty dip for carrots and celery.
- Chill out! Put grapes, fresh pineapple, or a peeled banana in the freezer to create a healthy frozen treat for a hot day.
- Play with your food! Try making a snack that is a work of art. Make animal shapes or flowers with your fruits and veggies, and then gobble them up.
- Mix it up! Skip the store-bought snacks and make your own snack mix out of low-fat, low-salt goodies that you enjoy.

Who said nutritious eating has to be boring?

The Majestic Bald Eagle

by Janet Hudgens

Suffix *-ion*

adoption	inscription	protection
extinction	legislation	suggestions
illustration	population	

Since 1782, the bald eagle has been the national bird of the United States. The year 1782 was also the year of the adoption of the Great Seal, the official emblem of the nation. The seal has an illustration of an eagle with its wings spread wide. In front of its body is a shield with thirteen red-and-white stripes. Above the eagle are thirteen white stars on a blue background. The eagle carries an olive branch—a symbol of peace—in one talon and thirteen arrows in the other. In its beak, it carries a banner that has the inscription *E pluribus unum*. That is Latin for "Out of many, one."

Before the eagle was chosen for the Great Seal, there were suggestions for other animals to appear on the seal. People suggested a rattlesnake, a dove, a rooster, and even a turkey. So why did the eagle make the final cut?

Bald eagles are considered very majestic and strong. The founders of the nation saw bald eagles as a symbol of freedom as they soared high above the land. Also, bald eagles are native to North America and were thought to live only on this continent. There is also a legend that the noise of a Revolutionary War battle awakened nearby eagles. The eagles began to shriek and soar above the battle. The colonial troops saw this as a sign that the eagles, too, were crying out for freedom.

The Great Seal and the symbol of the bald eagle appear in many places: on money, on buildings, on postage stamps, and on official stationery for the government. You can see it on the one dollar bill. Take a peek next time you have one. The eagle also appears on the flags of some individual U.S. states, as well as on the seals of different departments of the U.S. government.

Despite its popularity as a symbol of the country, the bald eagle was threatened. The greatest danger to the eagle has come from humans. For a long time, farmers considered eagles a threat to their livestock, so they hunted and killed many eagles. Other people captured eagles as trophies to show off. By the 1940s, the eagle population had declined so much that it was in danger. In 1940, the U.S. government passed legislation to protect these animals from hunting. But a ban on hunting was no longer enough protection. That is because a pesticide called DDT was in wide use. When eagles and other birds ate animals that had this poisonous chemical in their bodies, the birds started laying eggs that had extremely soft, fragile shells. The shells often broke before the young could hatch. Fewer and fewer eagles were being hatched and growing to adulthood. By the 1960s, there were fewer than 450 pairs of nesting adult eagles. The bald eagle was on the edge of extinction.

The use of DDT was banned in the 1970s, and eagles were protected as an endangered species. Soon their population began to grow again. In 2007 the bald eagle was removed from the list of endangered and threatened species. This majestic national symbol was once again safe.

Cleaning Southport Beach

by Andrew Goldsby

Suffix *-ion*

action	dedication	protection
celebration	motivation	starvation
collection	pollution	suffocation
complications		

Kaylee was so sad when she saw the beach. Usually a day at the beach was a real treat, but something was wrong today. People had left garbage all over the beach. Kaylee knew that this kind of pollution was not just ugly, but it could hurt the wildlife too. Plastic bags and packaging could be eaten by animals. This could cause complications in their digestive systems, leading to starvation. Animals also get entangled in plastic products, which can hinder their movements or cause suffocation. Protecting the animals and getting back her favorite beach was a big motivation for Kaylee to take action.

Kaylee asked her mom if they could work on cleaning up the garbage. They called some friends who also cared about the protection of the beach to help them. They stopped at the store for gloves and garbage bags. By the time they got back to the beach, several friends had arrived with their families. Organizing for the cleanup was really easy. Everyone just grabbed a bag and a pair of gloves, and the collection of garbage began.

Their dedication paid off. After two hours of cleaning, the workers had collected six bags of garbage, and Southport Beach was beautiful again. The cleanup crew decided a celebration was in order, but they wanted to set an example for others who would use the beach in the future. Kaylee's mom bought a sweet, juicy watermelon, which they cut up and ate on the beach, talking, laughing, and relaxing together after the hard work. Then they carefully packed up their garbage and took it home with them, leaving behind a spotless stretch of sand ready for enjoyment by everyone.

Sushi

by Caroline Richards

Suffix *-ion*

contamination	preparation	reaction
digestion	presentation	selection

If you have never had sushi, you might expect it to be kind of gross: raw fish, seaweed . . . ewww! However, your reaction might be different if you knew about the wide variety of sushi. It is considered quite healthy and is also quite tasty.

Sushi is a Japanese specialty. Basically, it is flavored rice with a selection of different ingredients added, such as vegetables, eggs, fish, or meat. The sticky rice might be pressed into a shape. This is called *nigiri sushi*. It might be rolled up tightly in thin sheets of seaweed paper. This is called *maki sushi*. The fish and other ingredients may be laid on top of the rice, pressed in with the rice, or tucked into the middle of the rolls. Sushi is always served cold, and almost always with a green horseradish paste called wasabi and some pickled ginger to aid digestion. Be careful when you eat these. Both can be a bit spicy!

Sushi is almost an art form. Chefs in sushi restaurants make their sushi very carefully. They want it to be not only delicious but also beautiful. The presentation on the plate is often very colorful and interesting. It is also very important that sushi with raw fish and seafood be prepared when the fish is freshest so that there is no contamination by bacteria.

Sushi restaurants are now very popular all over the world. If you ever get the chance, give sushi a try. You may discover a new favorite!

Celebrate Pretzels!

by Grace Ryan

Words from German

bagels	frankfurter	strudel
delicatessens	pretzel(s)	

April 26 is a holiday everyone can celebrate. It is the unofficial but still quite fun National Pretzel Day! No one quite knows how this holiday came to be or why. Yet, people across the United States actually celebrate it by baking, buying, sharing, and, of course, eating pretzels.

Traditional pretzels are not the crunchy twists and sticks you can buy in a bag. Those are a modern American invention. No, real pretzels are big, twisted rolls of bread. They are soft on the inside, a little crunchy on the outside, and baked to a rich brown color. They usually have a shiny coating of egg and a sprinkling of salt or seasonings. These proper pretzels don't come in plastic bags. You have to buy them fresh from pretzel stands, German bakeries, or delicatessens. Better yet, you can learn to make these delicious treats at home. There is nothing like a homemade pretzel fresh from the oven!

Pretzels, like other yummy baked goods such as strudel and bagels, were brought to the United States from Germany. Originally, pretzels were shaped into the familiar knot. In fact, that knotted bread was once a common symbol for German bakeries, and some still have them on their signs. The name *pretzel* actually comes from a Latin word meaning "little arms." That is because the pretzel knot looks like the crossed arms of a person. However, pretzels do come in other shapes, such as rolls and twists. Traditionally pretzels were eaten with sausage and mustard. Now you can find pretzels with a variety of other flavors and ways of eating them. Some Germans eat giant soft pretzels for breakfast. Others use pretzel rolls to make sandwiches. A new twist on an old idea is to wrap a rope of pretzel dough around a frankfurter and bake it. Then you have a pretzel-dog!

You and your family can easily make pretzels at home. The most basic recipes only call for yeast, water, sugar, flour, salt, and butter. The dough is rolled into long ropes. Those ropes are then twisted into the proper shape. The hardest part is actually getting those pretzel knots just right, but that's no cause for concern. It takes practice, even for experienced bakers, to produce a presentable pretzel knot. However, you'll find that even pretzels with crooked knots are yummy treats!

Pretzels are usually dipped into a mixture of water and baking soda or another substance before baking. This makes them cook just right, giving the pretzels their characteristic color and crisp crust.

Once your pretzels are baked, you have to decide whether you will sprinkle a topping on them. Often pretzels just have coarse salt sprinkled on them. You could also try grated cheeses, Italian herbs, or sunflower seeds. For something sweet, try toasted coconut or shaved dark chocolate. The choices are almost endless.

When April 26 rolls around again, be sure to celebrate with a big, fresh pretzel of your own!

Junior Teacher Day

by Annese Clark

Words from German

hamster	kindergartner	prattling
kindergarten	knapsack	

Every spring, fourth and fifth graders at Dillard Elementary school had the opportunity to sign up for Junior Teacher Day. Selected students would work with a teacher to prepare a lesson to share with one of the kindergarten classes at the school. Jonas had looked forward to this all year. He wanted to be a teacher someday, and he thought this would be a great experience.

Ms. Reynolds talked with Jonas about his lesson as the day drew near. He wanted to teach about taking care of pets. He was going to bring his hamster Morris and talk about all the chores he had to do to keep Morris healthy and happy. Ms. Reynolds thought this would be a fun lesson for the kindergartners to hear, and they would enjoy seeing Morris too.

Jonas brought Morris in his travel cage, along with a knapsack filled with the supplies he needed for his hamster. The younger children were very excited about Morris and interested in the lesson, especially those children who had or wanted pets of their own. Jonas felt like he was prattling, because he was nervous giving his lesson. But Ms. Reynolds smiled encouragingly, and he finished the lesson he had prepared.

As he returned to his own classroom after the lesson, he laughed about how hard that seemed. He had taught a lesson for 15 minutes, but his teacher had to teach all day every day. That must be a ton of planning, he thought to himself. If he was going to be a teacher, he'd have to get used to a lot more work!

Nick's Pup

by Lyla Zimmerman

Words from German

dachshund	plundered	rucksack
hamburger		

The room was a complete disaster. Nick's rucksack had been pulled off the bed, and the beef jerky that had been in it had been plundered and was gone forever. Nick knew who the culprit was. It was his dachshund puppy Boris.

Boris was a cute little pup, but Nick had some serious pet-owner anxiety. Boris was feisty and loud, and he tore up shoes and ate papers. He hunted for food all over Nick's room. He had occasional accidents that Nick had to clean up. It was time, Nick decided, to get Boris to behave better. Mom and Dad were in complete agreement.

On Saturday morning, Nick took Boris to dog obedience school. There were four other dogs and their owners there, but none were quite as wild as Boris. All morning long, Nick tried to get Boris to listen to commands, and all morning long, Boris barked and bounded around. The instructor said he just needed some practice.

Another week came and went with the same result, leaving Nick frustrated. The next week, the instructor gave the dog owners a tip about rewarding the dogs for good behavior. He suggested giving them a little bit of hamburger meat after each successful command. Nick tried that tip during the week, and since Boris liked nothing better than hamburger, it worked like a dream! Soon, Boris was calmly stopping, sitting, and even rolling over in order to earn his reward. Eventually the hamburger meat was unnecessary, though Nick still tried to give his puppy a treat when he was being especially good. Boris was a totally different dog. Nick was *very* relieved.

The Beggar and the Miser: An Arabian Folktale

Retold by Brent Fielding

Homographs

minute	produce	second
object(ed)	refuse(d)	subject(ed)

There was once a beggar who passed through an old village. He was an object of pity to many, for he had old shoes on his feet and only rags for clothes. He knocked on the door of a house that was big and beautiful. The grounds had a tall barn and a fancy iron gate. He guessed from the size of the barn that this house belonged to a rich, successful farmer. He hoped that the farmer might give him some of the produce of his farm, perhaps some fresh fruit or cheese. The thought made his mouth water. The beggar could not have known what everyone in town knew: the owner of this house was well-known for the attribute of avarice, or greed. Though he was very rich, he had never helped another human being.

After a minute, the gate opened, and the rich miser peeked out. He took in every minute detail of the beggar's appearance, but the sight of this poor man could not produce any changes in the man's opinions. He would refuse to show pity to this beggar, as he always did when asked for help.

"Good evening, kind sir," the beggar began. "I am wondering if you might have some meat or milk to share with a poor traveler."

No one had ever attributed kindness to the rich man. He couldn't see any reason why anyone would start to do so now. "No, I haven't," he shouted. "Now go away!" And with that he slammed the door.

The beggar waited a second or two and then knocked a second time. The rich man opened the door angrily.

"Sir, if you just had some wheat or a few beans left over to give me, that would be so good of you," the beggar said humbly.

The rich man objected very much to being made the object of this man's pathetic begging, for the suffering of poor people was a subject he particularly disliked. "I don't have anything!" the miser yelled before closing the door again.

The beggar was very hungry, and because of his great hunger, he subjected himself to the shame of asking yet again. He knocked a third time to see if he could get the man to show any pity.

"Sir, if you could spare even one piece of bread, I would be so grateful," the poor man said when the door was opened again.

"I don't have any bread!" the rich man shouted, and once again the door was slammed closed.

The beggar was ready to give up, but he was tired and thirsty. Surely, he thought, a farmer like this must have a well where he could get a drink. He knocked one last time.

"Sir, may I at least have just a drink of water, for it is very hot and I am dying of thirst?" he said when the owner had opened the door.

"I don't have any water!" the miser declared.

The beggar felt sorry for the miser, even though he had treated the beggar like refuse. "Oh, my unfortunate friend," cried the poor man in pity. "You have no meat, no beans, no grain, no bread, and no water. It is not me who should be begging but you, for you are poorer than I am!" And so he continued on his journey, leaving the miser to consider how little he deserved the pity of the poor, hungry beggar.

Camels: Ships of the Desert

by Rebecca Westphal

Homographs

desert   hide(s)   subject

For thousands of years, desert dwellers have relied on camels. These amazing animals are not just a source of transportation and a means of carrying loads. They also provide milk, meat, wool, and hides. Camels have been called "ships of the desert" because of their ability to cross hot sands with apparent ease. How do camels thrive where other animals can hardly survive?

Camels have some amazing adaptations that keep them alive in harsh deserts. Camels have hooves that are specially adapted to walk on the burning sands. Thick eyelashes hide their eyes and keep blowing sand and harsh sunlight from blinding them. Camels also have an ability to survive on drier plants that other livestock cannot use, such as thorns. Cattle and goats have to frequent the pastureland near an oasis, where water keeps the plants moist. However, camels can temporarily desert the flock to forage farther from the oasis. Camels are also not subject to the same dangers of dehydration that other mammals are. They do not sweat much at all, and they store water and nutrients in the tissues of their distinctive humps.

On the subject of humps, the two main kinds of camels can be easily distinguished by the humps on their backs. The Arabian camel, also called a dromedary, has one hump. The Bactrian camel has two humps.

There are almost no wild camels; they have been domesticated, which means they have been born and raised to be with humans. These beasts are great helpers in the heat of the desert.

Westward in the Wagon Train

by Jaime Bell

Homographs

compact(ed)	record	train
produce(d)	spring	

Jimmy peeked out from the back of their wagon as it bumped along. He and his sisters sat on top of the boxes, furniture, and mattresses. This compact wagon held everything their family owned in the whole world, compacted into the space of a small room. He stared through the clouds of dust produced by the slow-moving wooden wheels. What he saw was dozens of wagons just like his. Jimmy and his family were part of a wagon train heading west to new opportunities in Oregon.

In the late 1800s and much of the 1900s, wagon trains brought thousands of settlers to new lives in the West. These trains consisted of as many as a hundred wagons. They were often very organized, with set times for starting and stopping each day. Elected leaders made decisions for the group along the way. Families would pay a little to join a wagon train in order to have the help of guides and the company of other people on the way.

Traveling in such large numbers added to everyone's safety. It also helped make the trip more convenient. Settlers would share responsibilities for setting up camp, cooking, and guarding the wagons. They shared supplies, even produce if they could find it. They would keep each other company in the evenings.

About 500,000 people made the 2,000-mile journey from Missouri to California or the West by wagon. Many of them left records of their journeys. They would leave when the weather got nice in the spring. If they had good weather and no accidents, they would finally arrive about five months later. The journey was hard, but many people took it to follow a dream and the promise of a better life.

Pioneer Picnic

by Martin Kimberlin

Latin Roots *gener* and *port*

general	generation(s)	portable
generally	generous	transporting
generated	important	

Mr. McKinney generally found it pretty easy to get the attention of his class. This day was no exception. Mr. McKinney walked in wearing dusty canvas overalls, an old hat, and big boots. He had a bandanna tied around his neck and a garden rake propped on his shoulder. He took the piece of straw that he was chewing out of his mouth and looked around the room.

"Howdy, young'uns," he said with a drawl. "We're aimin' to have ourselves a working next week, and y'all are mighty welcome to come and help a bit. We'll have some good home-cooked vittles when we're all done." The funny accent and strange clothes generated some giggles. Then Mr. McKinney put down his tool, took off his hat, and explained his strange appearance.

"We have been studying pioneer times this week," he said. "Next week we're going to take a closer look at pioneer life. Pioneer families had to work hard, but they found that if they shared the work, the task was easier for everyone. For example, when someone needed a new barn, families from miles around might come to help build it. But these gatherings, sometimes called workings, weren't all work. It gave these families a chance to enjoy time together too. They would usually eat together and then have some music and dancing in the evenings. Every generation, from the youngest child to the oldest adult, found something to enjoy."

There was a dramatic pause, and the students wondered what was coming next.

"As you know," Mr. McKinney continued, "we are starting a student garden for the spring, and there's some important work to do to get it ready. So we are going to have a working to get it done. When we finish, we'll enjoy a genuine pioneer picnic. How does that sound?"

There was general agreement that this was going to be great fun. Mr. McKinney passed out information for students to share with their parents about this special project.

Tuesday came quickly, and the bright sun promised a perfect day for the project. All the students, in old clothes and shoes, worked hard transporting soil, seeds, water buckets, and mulch to the garden area. Ms. Kiama, the principal, told them about the flowers and vegetables that would be grown there.

As it got close to noon, Ms. Kiama declared that the garden was finished. She sent the students inside to wash their hands. Some of the students helped her spread picnic blankets on the ground while others assisted Mr. McKinney in carrying out the portable pioneer feast. There were generous helpings of cornbread and biscuits with fresh butter and fruity jam. There were cold chicken legs, ham sandwiches, a big pot of pinto beans, and corn on the cob. And best of all, there were the reddest strawberries the students had ever seen and real raspberry juice and homemade lemonade to refresh everyone after their hard, hot work in the garden.

Then, just as with the workings in past generations, a catchy tune on a harmonica made everyone's toes tap. Mr. McKinney really knew how to plan a picnic!

Along the Silk Road

by Marilee Snyder

Latin Roots *gener* and *port*

exported	generations	portable
generally	imported	transported
generate		

Long before airplanes, long before cars, long before even sailing ships could make the long trip between China and Rome, those two cultures were connected. Goods were being transported and traded regularly between them. Those goods were carried along what came to be known as the Silk Road.

The Silk Road was not actually a single road, but rather a series of trade routes that connected two empires. These routes passed through parts of what is now China, Afghanistan, India, Iran, Iraq, Turkey, and other places. Traders did not usually travel the whole 4,000-plus mile route. It was a dangerous and difficult journey. They had to go across deserts, over mountains, and through bandit-plagued regions. Groups of traders would generally move together between trading towns and outposts. They exchanged whatever they happened to have for new products to carry back home and generate profits.

Many portable treasures moved along the Silk Road. Romans, and later other Europeans, imported the beautiful silks and delicious spices from the East. They exported wool, gold, and silver to China and other places along the way. Ideas and knowledge were also imported and exported along the Silk Road. Generations of travelers and traders learned about other peoples and their fascinating cultures. The Silk Road opened the world up and brought diverse cultures closer together.

A Mayflower Child

by Cassandra Ho

Latin Roots *gener* and *port*

generally	generation	transportation
generated	important	transported

The journey had taken two months. Many people were sick and weak after the hard voyage. At first, Samuel had been excited at the thought of life in a new land. He had stood on the deck of the *Mayflower* and waved goodbye to his old home. But there had been delays, and they had traveled during the stormy season. That kind of transportation was very unpleasant. Now Samuel was ready to be on solid ground.

Samuel, his father, and the other colonists landed at Cape Cod late in 1620. While they made homes and prepared for life in the colony, they had to stay on the smelly, uncomfortable ship. This generated a few complaints, but there was nothing that could be done about it.

At last, the colonists transported their things to the shore and moved into the homes they had prepared, but the hard times weren't over. Many people got sick, and everyone was hungry. Generally, the children were the healthiest colonists that year, and they had to take on a lot of responsibility. Samuel helped carry water and chop firewood, and he had to learn to cook simple meals. At the end of the second winter, there were only a few dozen colonists still alive.

One day, Samuel saw a tall, proud native man walk into their tiny village. Samuel stopped doing his chores to watch this man as he spoke with the village leaders. His name, Samuel learned later, was Samoset, and he spoke English well. He offered to help them get some of the food and tools they needed.

Samoset kept his promise and brought them the help they needed. Samuel knew the colony at Plymouth would survive for his generation, thanks to this important friendship.

The Mystery of Oak Island

by Katelyn McNab

Oak Island

Nova Scotia

Latin Roots *dur* and *ject*

dejected	endured	objects
durable	objective	project
duration		

On tiny Oak Island in Nova Scotia, Canada, a mystery has endured for more than 200 years. In 1795, a young man named Daniel McGinnis went fishing on the island. He found a tree with strange markings and an area of ground that looked like it might have been dug up. The next day he came back with two friends. Their objective was to dig up the treasure Daniel thought must be buried there.

For the duration of the weekend, the three friends dug into the ground. They got very excited when they found some objects, such as paving stones and cut logs. But after hours of digging without success, they became dejected and gave up for a time.

However, Daniel and his friends never forgot the unusual dig. Nine years later the three friends returned to try again. With the help of others, they came with more equipment and money to complete their project, or so they thought.

They began digging again and got even deeper than before. They found more objects that didn't seem to belong: coconut fibers, bricks, and a stone carved with what appeared to be a code. They thought surely the treasure must be close, but more digging only uncovered more logs. Disappointed, they stopped for the weekend.

When they returned Monday morning, the entire shaft was flooded with seawater. The digging was abandoned, but the treasure-hunters planned to continue the project in the spring. None of the efforts they made worked, and eventually they ran out of money. The legendary Oak Island treasure remained hidden.

Other groups tried to uncover the supposed treasure over the years. Several of them ran out of money, the same as the first group, or had other problems that caused them to abandon the work. Bigger and more advanced equipment was brought in, more durable materials were used, and various theories were tested. Still, the digs kept flooding and collapsing, making it impossible to get to the bottom of this mysterious pit. Millions of dollars were poured into the work over the years. Some thought the pit must have been cleverly booby-trapped by the original creators to keep strangers out. Others began to believe that the pit was a natural occurrence called a sinkhole, and that these unnatural objects had washed into the hole in some kind of flood. Some thought it was just a really unlucky place.

Even in the 1900s and 2000s, work has continued, drawing such famous people as President Franklin D. Roosevelt and actor John Wayne to participate. Advanced technology has opened up new possibilities. A fiberoptic camera system was used to get pictures inside a sea cavern deep beneath the pit. The pictures show what seem to be wooden chests, digging tools, and skeletons. The pictures have kept alive the desire of treasure hunters to get to the bottom of the mystery and finally find what secrets Oak Island's pit really holds.

The Time Capsule

by Mia Michaels

Latin Roots dur and ject

durable	endured	project
during	object	rejected

Milo once read a magazine article about making a time capsule. The article suggested collecting things about yourself and your family and storing them away for a time period of twenty or thirty years. The writer described opening her own time capsule that she and her sister had made thirty years earlier. She said it was really fun to see how some of their likes, dislikes, and personality traits had endured through the years.

During dinner, Milo talked with his family about doing a project like this. They all agreed this was a great idea. They enthusiastically exchanged ideas about what to include in the time capsule.

Mom found a durable plastic box that they could use, and Milo brainstormed a list of things they each should put in the capsule. They included photos of family members and that morning's newspaper in the box. They included an advertisement from the electronics store to show what technology was available.

Each family member put in an object or two to represent a hobby or interest. Milo put in a stamp from his stamp collection. His brother Gabe put in a toy car that was like the model he was building. Dad put in his famous barbecue sauce recipe. Milo rejected the idea of putting in any real food because he didn't want it to spoil. Instead, they put in wrappers from some of their favorite snacks.

The final addition was a private letter from family members. They wrote about their dreams and wishes for themselves and their whole family. When the letters were in the box, they sealed it and wrote on top "Open in 2040." Now opening the time capsule was one thing they could definitely look forward to!

Movie Night

by Stephen Ford

Latin Roots *dur* and *ject*

duration	subject	unendurable
projector		

Bradley had been stuck in the house for a week because he had had emergency surgery to take out his appendix and was still not strong enough to go out. The boredom was almost unendurable for an active boy like Bradley. Besides, the first Friday of the month he usually went to the movies with his friends Darius and Beth. It was the first Friday, and he was sure they would be going to have fun without him. Bradley was in a pretty bad mood.

He asked to be excused from the table, saying he thought he would go lay in bed and read until bedtime. His mother raised her eyebrows, as though she thought he was doing something especially odd.

"I thought this was your movie night," she said.

It was a subject that only irritated him, since he couldn't go out. "I don't care," he said glumly.

111

"That's a shame," his mother said with a mysterious smile. "Darius and Beth are going to be disappointed."

Just then, the doorbell rang. A minute later, his mother returned to the dining room with his best friends following her.

"What are you guys doing here?" Bradley asked, surprised.

"We're here for movie night!" Darius declared.

A few minutes later, they were settled in the basement, where Bradley's mother had created their own private movie theater. She had set up a projector so they could see the movie on the "big screen," and she had a big bowl of popcorn waiting for them. It was a great surprise to be able to have movie night without leaving the house. Bradley was in an excellent mood for the duration of the evening.

The Great Escape

by Beth Jordain

Words from French

alarm	danger	hazards
blanket	guard	patrol
companions		

Dusty was sound asleep, wrapped in a blanket with his feet pointed toward the dying campfire. He always slept hard after a long day on the trail. They had already been on the trail for ten days, and he was dreaming of the soft bed, warm bath, and hot meals that awaited him when they got to Amarillo.

Suddenly the sound of coyotes howling awoke him and the other cowhands. The horses shifted their feet restlessly, and the cattle began lowing in alarm. Coyotes were one of the hazards of a cattle trail. Occasionally these hunters would attack a herd and try to get one or two of the cows.

Another chorus of howls sounded even closer, and the cowhands sprang into action. They jumped on their horses and went to see about the cows. They were nervous and jumpy because of the coyotes. Dusty and his friends needed to keep the cattle close so they could protect them from the predators in the wild. They began to patrol the edges of the herd, trying to coax the cattle to move farther into the little canyon where they had made their camp.

The coyotes howled a third time, and this was too much for some of the more skittish cows. A little group of them scattered and ran away. Dusty knew that these wandering cows were in much more danger by themselves. Quickly, Dusty called a couple of his companions to help him round up the escapees, while the others stayed to guard the remaining herd.

It was still the middle of the night, and the darkness was thick. This created yet another danger: The frightened cattle or the cowboys' horses could stumble into a crack or hole and injure themselves badly. Dusty guided his horse carefully to where he heard a couple of the runaway cows moving around.

Cowhands kept lassos on their saddles so they had the ropes when needed.

Dusty could see the cow and the calf with her by the faint light of the half-moon that still remained in the night sky. They were still frightened and trying frantically to scramble up a little hill. The rocks and dirt there were loose, and the poor cow was stumbling and slipping, which made her even more frantic.

Slowly, Dusty drew near, speaking calmly to the frightened animal. He did not dare come too close, because her nervous movements could cause her to hurt him or herself. Instead, he let out his rope and prepared to throw it. The lasso landed gently over the cow's head, and he drew it gently tighter so he could guide her down from the little slope. It took a minute to get her to stop fighting the rope, but soon she calmed enough to let Dusty lead her toward him. He patted her head gently to soothe her. He fastened another rope to the calf and attached both ropes to his saddle.

Dusty met up with the other cowhands on the way back to camp. Each of the others also led a cow or two. By the time they returned to the herd, the sky was beginning to get light. The other cowhands had put away their bedrolls and blankets and were getting cooking fires started for breakfast. Soon the herd was back together and ready to move on down the trail.

In the Okefenokee Swamp

by Michael Brothers

Words from French

inhabit	precise	variety
native	refuge	

You may think that getting stuck in a swamp is the last thing you would want to do, but think again! A visit to the Okefenokee Swamp, which covers more than 600 square miles in Georgia and Florida, can be a fascinating, fun experience. Seeing the diverse wildlife and strange, shifting landscape is worth the trip.

Okefenokee is a Native American word that has been translated as "Trembling Earth," but some people argue that a more precise translation would be "Trembling Water." The shifting swamp islands and waterways make either one an accurate description.

In 1937, a large part of the swamp was designated as the Okefenokee National Wildlife Refuge. This has helped to protect the many species of animals that inhabit the swamp. More than 170 species of birds make their home there. So do bears, deer, raccoons, otters, and a huge variety of insects, amphibians, and other critters.

The diversity doesn't end with the animals. Trees, vines, and water plants fill the swamp, and exotic flowers add splashes of color to the lush greens. Floating islands covered with trees and plants are an interesting phenomenon in this remarkable place.

Boat trips are a great way to see the Okefenokee. While you are out, keep an eye on the water to catch sight of the main attraction: alligators. These stars of the swamp are common sights. Just keep your eyes open— and your hands and feet inside the boat!

Animal Art

by Jake Lindsey

Words from French

accidentally	dozens	ruined
apartment	enjoy	technique
community	palette	unique
company	paper	

Casey had stumbled on her favorite way of painting accidentally. She was trying to paint a mural on her studio wall one day, and she had a palette of paints sitting on the floor beside her. Without warning, her golden retriever, Trevor, had come bounding into the room. He ran through the paint and then leaped up to greet her, leaving sloppy, colorful paw prints on her new T-shirt. The shirt was ruined . . . but a new technique had been born.

Still in her newly painted T-shirt, Casey found a large roll of paper and covered the floor with it. Then she poured a little paint in a shallow pan and tried to coax Trevor to step through it again. The playful pup figured out fast that this was a game he would enjoy. He jumped into the paint again. Casey threw a rubber ball for him to chase. For each throw, she used a different color. The result was a bit messy. But she and Trevor had so much fun that they kept going.

Trevor had to get used to taking baths on paint days, but otherwise he liked playing this way. Casey soon had dozens of unique paw print paintings. Her studio was filled with them. So was her apartment.

Her town had an outdoor art fair every spring, so Casey decided to rent a booth there and share her cheerful paintings with the community. Trevor, who came to keep her company in the booth, drew a large crowd. By the end of the weekend, Casey had sold all but three of the paintings! Trevor's masterpieces were a big hit.

Becoming a Butterfly

by Brian Bridges

Related Words

beautiful/beauty

developed/
developing/
development

final/finally

grow/grown/
growth/outgrow

larva(e)/
larval

lovely/
unlovely

pupa/pupal

transformation/
transforming

winged/wingless/
wings

Every butterfly begins life as a tiny egg. The female butterfly lays her eggs with a lot of care. Almost every species of butterfly has a particular plant that the butterflies prefer, and it is on these plants that the female will deposit eggs.

Before long, a tiny larva—called a caterpillar— emerges from the egg. If you have ever seen a caterpillar, you know that they look nothing like their winged parents. The chubby, wingless caterpillar can be quite unlovely compared to the graceful creature it will become. Caterpillars will go through several stages as they become fully grown butterflies.

121

The gradual transformation begins even in the larval stage. A caterpillar's main activity is eating, eating, and eating some more. It eats all the time! Larvae have very well-developed chewing mechanisms to handle all the eating they do. The larva needs lots of nutrients for its rapid growth. Some caterpillars can consume several times their body weight every day. Caterpillars outgrow their own skins several times. They molt, or shed off old skins as they grow new ones. Besides getting bigger, a caterpillar's appearance will also change as it gets bigger. The changes help it blend in with its surroundings to hide from predators.

After a while, the caterpillar is finally ready for another stage of development, called a pupa. During the pupal stage, the caterpillar attaches itself to a stem or leaf and molts for the last time. The final skin turns into a shell called the chrysalis. It may seem that the pupal stage is a time of rest, since there is no activity visible on the outside. But inside that chrysalis an incredible transformation is going on. Wings are developing. The chewing parts of the mouth are turning into the proboscis (the long, nectar-sucking snout) of a butterfly. The antennae that help it explore its world are emerging. The body is transforming, getting ready for flight. The pupal stage lasts for anywhere from 10 to 14 days.

When that work is done, an adult butterfly emerges from that shell. The wings aren't ready for flight right away. In fact, they appear a little shriveled when the butterfly first emerges. But the wings "plump up" as water is pushed out from the body and into the wings. As the enlarged wings dry, the butterfly will prepare for flight. Finally, the butterfly spreads its lovely wings and begins to explore the world from a new perspective. The new butterfly goes in search of a mate. Soon the cycle begins all over again.

It might be hard to actually observe all these stages, but you could enjoy the beauty of butterflies by planting a butterfly garden at home. Ask at a plant nursery or botanical garden about good plants to attract beautiful butterflies to your garden.

The Great American Bake Sale

by Nicole Inrig

Related Words

bake/baked/ baker(s)/bakery

generosity/ generous

hunger/hungry

neighborhood/ neighbors

organize/ organized/ organizers

support/ supporters/ supportive

Jen saw a news report about a neighborhood bake sale that was raising money to help hungry children. It was part of a program called the Great American Bake Sale. This program encourages people to organize bake sales as fundraisers. There were so many neighbors involved that it took four tables to hold the baked goods. More than two hundred customers had come to support the bakers and buy the baked treats. Jen was impressed both by how well the sale was organized and by how the organizers and supporters were so interested in fighting hunger.

Jen was a good baker, and so were her mom and aunts. What a great way to have some special family time and draw the neighborhood together! She decided to organize a Great American Bake Sale herself.

The first step was to pick a day and place. Then she invited her friends and neighbors to participate. She was amazed by the generous responses she got. Nearly every neighbor agreed enthusiastically to make something. Some volunteered to bring tables and chairs, while others called their friends to be involved. Jen contacted the local newspaper and radio stations about advertising the bake sale, and they all offered to do it free of charge. The family kitchen was turned into a full-time bakery. Anyone who had some spare time was recruited to run to the store for extra ingredients, stir batter, check the oven, or package the finished treats.

The sale was a huge success, and Jen was thrilled by the generosity of all the people who stopped for the sale. Hundreds of rolls, breads, muffins, and treats were purchased by the supportive customers. Many people also donated additional money for the cause. When the day was over, Jen and her neighbors had collected $1,200, a sweet return!

From Seed to Sunflower

by Jasmine Wright

Related Words

locate/location

plant/plantable/
planted/planter(s)/
planting/transplant

seed(s)/seedling

sun/sunflower(s)/
sunlight/sunny

Bright and cheerful, sunflowers are a fun and easy plant to grow. To start them inside, you will need one or more containers for planting and some potting soil. Of course, you also need sunflower seeds, but make sure you have plantable seeds, not the kind you eat.

Cover your work area with some newspaper. Fill each planter about two-thirds full with potting soil. With your finger or a pencil, poke a little hole in the soil and drop a seed into the hole. Carefully cover the seed with soil, but don't press down too firmly. When your seeds are all planted, gently sprinkle water over the soil. It should be moist, not super-wet. Place the planters in a sunny location and leave them there. Check them regularly to make sure the soil is damp, and water them as necessary.

After a few days, you will see a tiny green stem poking through the soil. Your seed is turning into a seedling. When this little stem is a couple of inches tall, it is time to move your plant outside. Locate a safe, sunny spot where your plant can get used to being outdoors. After a day or two you can transplant the seedling. As their name suggests, sunflowers really like the sun! Pick a place that receives a lot of sunlight. With a small trowel, dig a hole for your sunflower. Carefully loosen the soil around your seedling. Lift it out of the container and move it to the newly dug hole. Gently pat the soil back in place around your seedling and water it one more time. Then sit back and get ready to watch your sunflower grow!

My Trip to the Moon

by Julia Bowman

Greek Roots

astronaut(s)	astrophysics	atmosphere
astronautical	astrotourism	photographs
astronautics		

We had been saving up for a moon vacation for a long time. My sister Liana and I had done extra chores for three months to get some spending money for the trip. When Dad came home with the astrotourism brochure a few months ago, I was skeptical. We had talked about this vacation for so long that it seemed as though it would never happen. Dad was completely serious this time. Two days later, our tickets on the moon shuttle had been purchased, and we had reservations at a space resort called Lunar Landing.

Mom had heard that some people experienced space sickness on their first trip to space, so she had us drinking vitamin-filled "space smoothies." We had to think carefully about what to pack. Our regular Earth clothes would be fine on board the moon shuttle. We decided to just rent spacesuits when we got there.

Finally the day arrived for us to board the moon shuttle. Some of the astronauts were there to greet us and show us around. We weren't allowed in the cockpit, of course, but they showed us some of their labs and equipment. I really never knew how many buttons, switches, and knobs you needed on a spaceship. As the takeoff time drew near, we got seated and strapped into our seats in the specially pressurized passenger cabin. Then three, two, one, ignition! We took off, literally, like a rocket! Even with the pressure being carefully controlled, I could feel the force of gravity pressing on me and the ship as we left the atmosphere. And then, suddenly, the pressure lifted and we were in space.

The trip to the moon was expected to take about three days. Ordinarily, I am not that patient, but there was so much for passengers to do on the moon shuttle that I was afraid I wouldn't have enough time to do it all. They had movies and even bowling for people who were a little homesick for Earth. The ship had a fascinating museum of astronautics, which contained photographs and equipment from every major space mission since the 1960s. There was also a low-gravity practice chamber, which Mom insisted that we visit every morning to get ready for the reduced gravity of the moon. Dad took me with him to a lecture on astrophysics one morning. I expected it to be boring, but it actually turned out to be pretty exciting. The best part, though, was the junior astronaut club, where we met the real astronauts again and learned more about their training and equipment.

That amazing flight came to an end much too quickly. Soon, we were preparing for our transfer to the moon bus, which would carry us from our orbit around the moon down to the resort on the surface. I was sure the moon vacation was going to be great, but I couldn't help being a little sad to leave the shuttle. I looked forward to the return trip and the chance for another astronautical adventure.

Capturing the Stars

by Wes Brooks

Greek Roots

astrodynamics	astronomy	photographs
astronomer	astrophotography	telescope

Samuel had astronomy on the brain, or at least that is what his grandfather said. At night, if he wasn't looking at the stars through his telescope, he was dreaming about stars in his sleep. He imagined a day when he would proudly announce that he had discovered a new planet.

His grandfather had been an amateur astronomer too. He had grown up in an era when rockets and satellites were just reaching into space, and he kept his telescope pointed at the sky. His daughter, Samuel's aunt Carolyn, had also fallen in love with the stars. She went to college to study astrodynamics, which is the study of how stars and other space bodies move and affect one another. She worked at an observatory in California, watching the skies and recording the details she saw. She had given Samuel the telescope he loved so much and taught him how to best use it.

Samuel's visit to the space observatory where Carolyn worked turned his interest in a surprising new direction. One of her colleagues had some amazing photographs of space bodies and events. One photograph showed an enormous cloud of gases called a nebula. Another photograph showed the dense cluster of stars that surrounded the center of the Milky Way. Another was a time-lapse picture of the stars above the observatory, which looked like a million little streaks of light because of the rotation of the Earth. He explained that these were examples of astrophotography, which used special cameras attached to telescopes to capture pictures of the heavens. Samuel decided that that was what he wanted to do: combine science and art to explore the wonder of the stars.

Flight into History

by Rob Ledger

Greek Roots

aeronautical	astrionics	astronautical
aeronautics	astronaut	
aerospace		

Mission Specialist Guion S. Bluford ran through his checklists in preparation for takeoff. This mission on board the *Challenger* space shuttle was his first space mission. It was another first as well. On August 30, 1983, Guion Bluford became the first African American in space.

Bluford knew quite early that he wanted to fly. In college he studied aerospace engineering. He was also in a training program to be an officer in the U.S. Air Force. He flew jets in the Air Force, and he earned a reputation as a skillful and brave pilot. After the Vietnam War, he served as an engineer and teacher as well as a pilot. He continued studying aerospace engineering, eventually getting a doctorate degree in 1978. He joined the National Aeronautics and Space Administration (NASA) to train as an astronaut that same year.

After the *Challenger* mission in 1983, Bluford participated in three other space missions. He was a mission specialist on each flight. He conducted experiments, launched satellites, and collected astronautical and aeronautical data. His training in engineering gave him special skills in astrionics, or electrical systems necessary for space flight. By the time he left NASA in 1993, he had spent more than 688 hours in space and orbited the Earth 458 times.

Guion Bluford didn't stop exploring after his years as an astronaut. He returned to school to study business, and then returned to a career in engineering.

Standing Up for the Skate Park

by Lynne Reitmeyer

The new skateboarding rules were totally unfair! For the third day in a row, a community officer had stopped her and her friends from practicing their tricks in the park. They had not been in anyone's way, and they were all trying to be as safe as possible, but the police officer told them that skateboards were not allowed in the park. It seemed as though skateboards weren't allowed anywhere. It was really hard for the neighborhood kids to find a place for their favorite activity.

At school the next day, her social studies teacher talked about civic rights and responsibilities. He said citizens always have the right and the ability to address community problems and to look for solutions. Yasmin felt he was talking *especially* about the way she was feeling, so she decided that she would bring her frustration to the city council.

Yasmin asked her teacher, Mr. Ramirez, for advice. He suggested that she write a polite letter explaining the problem and recommending a reasonable solution. Complaining wouldn't get their attention, Mr. Ramirez said, but offering a realistic solution would. Yasmin took his advice and began to write. She mailed the letter and waited.

Two weeks later a letter arrived. It was written on paper with the official seal of the local government on it. It looked very serious and important. Ms. Moria, the representative for her district of town, invited Yasmin to present her proposal at the next council meeting.

Yasmin realized that the city council was actually going to take her seriously. It felt like a lot of responsibility for one kid, but she knew she had the ability to share her passion this way.

Yasmin arrived for the meeting as early as possible and went over her presentation in her mind. When she was finally invited to speak, she shared her idea to turn the parking lot behind the old library into a skate park. She explained about the problem with the restrictions in the park and the ways a new skate park would serve the young people while also helping them learn to skate safely.

When she finished, Ms. Moria thanked her for coming and sharing her idea.

"Thank you for your honesty and creativity, Yasmin," she said. "You've shown a lot of maturity by explaining this need in our community and the realistic possibility for meeting it. As you know, we have a lot of things to consider, and we have to prioritize how we address them. However, we promise to consider your proposal very seriously."

Yasmin didn't know whether her efforts would produce a positive result, but she was optimistic. It was almost four months, though, before she found out the city council's decision. One day some construction vehicles set up a fence around the old library parking lot. A sign on the fence showed her success. It said, "Coming soon! Springbrook City Skate Park." Being a problem-solver instead of a complainer had paid off.

A History of Hoops

by Ann Lucado

> **Greek and Latin Suffixes**
>
> ability
>
> athleticism
>
> idolize
>
> improvements
>
> organized
>
> popularity
>
> refinements
>
> revolutionized
>
> undeniable

Put together ten players, two baskets, one bouncing ball, and one oblong court, and what do you have? You have basketball, the only sport that was invented in the United States.

The first basketball game took place on December 1, 1891, in Springfield, Massachusetts. It featured two fruit baskets as goals and a soccer ball. James Naismith, a physical education instructor, organized that first game and wrote the first official rules, publishing them less than two months later. By 1900, basketball was being played in places around the world.

Basketball continued to evolve over time. Refinements to the rules, changes in court sizes and shapes, and improvements in basketball hoops and balls revolutionized the game. At the same time, the game grew in popularity. Some players became very serious about this sport, and eventually professional basketball was born.

There is a lot of running, jumping, and shooting involved in this active sport. Players need a lot of natural ability, learned skills, and athleticism. It is undeniable that fans of all ages idolize basketball stars because of their extraordinary skills. Generations of kids in public parks, school playgrounds, physical education classes, and gyms have fallen in love with the game. They have James Naismith to thank for the all-American sport of basketball.

The Illusionist

by Gina Poulous

Greek and Latin Suffixes

amazement	equipment	realized
appointment	gullible	reliable
assortment	honesty	skepticism
compartments	illusionist	specialized
disappointment	impossible	unbelievable
enjoyment	incredibly	

Carlos watched the performance of Magnifico with mixed feelings. Magnifico called himself an illusionist. It was his job to make people believe the unbelievable, and he did it very well. Carlos was not gullible, and he realized these were all tricks. Still, he left the show in amazement at the impossible things the illusionist had done.

For days after the show, Carlos continued to wonder about the tricks. He wanted to find a reliable person to teach him the secrets behind the illusions. Who better than the great Magnifico himself? Carlos set up an appointment to talk to Magnifico the next afternoon.

Carlos experienced a moment of disappointment when Magnifico showed up in jeans and a T-shirt instead of his cape and top hat. Carlos politely expressed his desire to learn the truth about the illusions. Magnifico had experienced such skepticism before, but he appreciated Carlos's honesty. He agreed to give Carlos a lesson in the art of illusion.

Magnifico showed Carlos some of his favorite tricks. Carlos saw the assortment of wires, hidden compartments, and specialized equipment that made the illusions seem real. When the tour and lesson were over, Magnifico invited Carlos to come to that evening's show.

Carlos thought he might not have as much fun, now that he had seen some of Magnifico's secrets. The opposite was actually true. Knowing a few of the tricks increased his enjoyment, because he could see how incredibly skilled Magnifico really was.

Acknowledgments

Photographs:

1 Fotokostic/Shutterstock; **2** TAO XIYI/Xinhua/Landov; **9** Galyna Andrushko/Shutterstock; **11** ©Robin Weaver/Alamy; **17** ©Archive Images/Alamy; **20** ©Bettmann/CORBIS; **25** ©Heritage Images/Corbis; **27** SSPL/Getty Images; **33** Travel Photo by Steve McDonald/Getty Images; **35** ©North Wind Picture Archives/Alamy; **41** ©CORBIS; **43** ©H. Armstrong Roberts/CORBIS; **49** Michael Sewell/Peter Arnold/Getty Images; **51** ©INTERFOTO/Alamy; **58** (left) ©Eric Gaillard/Reuters/Corbis, (right) Hulton Archive/Getty Images; **66** Adam Taylor/Thinkstock; **67** Mike Flippo/Shutterstock; **73** ©lowthian/Fotolia; **74** ©Richard Laschon/Fotolia; **81** ©PackShot/Fotolia; **83** Paris L. Gray/Courier Post/Associated Press; **89** ©Pearson Education, Inc.; **91** ©Pearson Education, Inc.; **98** Durand, Asher Brown (1796–1886)/© Collection of the New-York Historical Society, USA/The Bridgeman Art Library; **100** ©Glow Images/Glow Botanica; **105** ©Pearson Education, Inc; **107** ©Pearson Education, Inc.; **113** ©North Wind Picture Archives/Alamy; **115** ©Don B. Stevenson/Alamy; **122** ©Universal Images Group Limited/Alamy; **124** ©Pavel Timofeev/Fotolia.com; **129** Richard T. Nowitz/Science Source; **131** Larry Landolfi/Photo Researchers/Getty Images; **137** ©Mike McGill/CORBIS; **139** ©ZUMA Press, Inc./Alamy.